VIOLIN

CHRISTMAS FAVORITES

Solos and String Orchestra Arrangements
Correlated with Essential Elements String Method

Arranged by
LLOYD CONLEY

Welcome to Essential Elements Christmas Favorites! There are two versions of each selection in this versatile book. The SOLO version appears in the beginning of your book. The STRING ORCHESTRA arrangements of each song follows. The supplemental recording (CD or Cassette) or string orchestra PIANO PART may be used as an accompaniment for solo performance. Use these recordings when playing solos for friends and family.

ISBN 978-0-7935-8391-1

HAL•LEONARD®
CORPORATION
7777 W. BLUEMOUND RD. P.O. BOX 13819 MILWAUKEE, WI 53213

00868011

JINGLE BELLS

VIOLIN
Solo

Words and Music by J. PIERPONT
Arranged by LLOYD CONLEY

UP ON THE HOUSETOP

VIOLIN
Solo

Words and Music by B.R. HANDY
Arranged by LLOYD CONLEY

THE HANUKKAH SONG

VIOLIN
Solo

Traditional
Arranged by LLOYD CONLEY

WE WISH YOU A MERRY CHRISTMAS

VIOLIN
Solo

Traditional English Folksong
Arranged by LLOYD CONLEY

A HOLLY JOLLY CHRISTMAS

VIOLIN
Solo

Music and Lyrics by JOHNNY MARKS
Arranged by LLOYD CONLEY

00868011

FROSTY THE SNOW MAN

**Words and Music by
STEVE NELSON and JACK ROLLINS**
Arranged by LLOYD CONLEY

VIOLIN
Solo

Fros - ty the snow man was a jol - ly hap - py
Fros - ty the snow man is a fair - y tale they

soul, With a corn cob pipe and a but - ton nose and two eyes made out of
say, He was made of snow, but the chil - dren know how he

coal. came to life one day. There must have been some

mag - ic in that old silk hat they found. For when they placed it

on his head he be - gan to dance a - round. Oh, Fros - ty the

snow man was a - live as he could be, And the chil - dren say he could

laugh and play just the same as you and me.

Thump - et - y thump thump, thump - et - y thump thump. Look at Frost - y go.

Thump - et - y thump thump, thump - et - y thump thump. O - ver the hills of snow.

ROCKIN' AROUND THE CHRISTMAS TREE

VIOLIN
Solo

Music and Lyrics by **JOHNNY MARKS**
Arranged by **LLOYD CONLEY**

Copyright © 1958 (Renewed 1986) St. Nicholas Music Inc., 1619 Broadway, New York, New York 10019
This arrangement Copyright © 1997 St. Nicholas Music Inc.
All Rights Reserved

JINGLE-BELL ROCK

VIOLIN
Solo

Words and Music by
JOE BEAL and JIM BOOTHE
Arranged by LLOYD CONLEY

00868011

SILVER BELLS
From the Paramount Picture THE LEMON DROP KID

VIOLIN
Solo

Words and Music by
JAY LIVINGSTON and RAY EVANS
Arranged by LLOYD CONLEY

LET IT SNOW! LET IT SNOW! LET IT SNOW!

Words by SAMMY CAHN
Music by JULE STYNE
Arranged by LLOYD CONLEY

VIOLIN
Solo

00868011

WHITE CHRISTMAS

From the Motion Picture Irving Berlin's HOLIDAY INN

VIOLIN
Solo

Words and Music by IRVING BERLIN
Arranged by LLOYD CONLEY

JINGLE BELLS

VIOLIN
String Orchestra Arrangement

Words and Music by J. PIERPONT
Arranged by LLOYD CONLEY

00868011

UP ON THE HOUSETOP

VIOLIN 1
String Orchestra Arrangement

Words and Music by B.R. HANDY
Arranged by LLOYD CONLEY

UP ON THE HOUSETOP

VIOLIN 2
String Orchestra Arrangement

Words and Music by B.R. HANDY
Arranged by LLOYD CONLEY

00868011

THE HANUKKAH SONG

VIOLIN 1
String Orchestra Arrangement

Traditional
Arranged by LLOYD CONLEY

THE HANUKKAH SONG

VIOLIN 2
String Orchestra Arrangement

Traditional
Arranged by LLOYD CONLEY

00868011

WE WISH YOU A MERRY CHRISTMAS

VIOLIN 1
String Orchestra Arrangement

Traditional English Folksong
Arranged by LLOYD CONLEY

WE WISH YOU A MERRY CHRISTMAS

VIOLIN 2
String Orchestra Arrangement

Traditional English Folksong
Arranged by LLOYD CONLEY

A HOLLY JOLLY CHRISTMAS

VIOLIN 1
String Orchestra Arrangement

Music and Lyrics by JOHNNY MARKS
Arranged by LLOYD CONLEY

A HOLLY JOLLY CHRISTMAS

VIOLIN 2
String Orchestra Arrangement

Music and Lyrics by JOHNNY MARKS
Arranged by LLOYD CONLEY

FROSTY THE SNOW MAN

Words and Music by
STEVE NELSON and JACK ROLLINS
Arranged by LLOYD CONLEY

VIOLIN 1
String Orchestra Arrangement

00868011

FROSTY THE SNOW MAN

Words and Music by
STEVE NELSON and **JACK ROLLINS**
Arranged by LLOYD CONLEY

VIOLIN 2
String Orchestra Arrangement

00868011

ROCKIN' AROUND THE CHRISTMAS TREE

VIOLIN 1
String Orchestra Arrangement

Music and Lyrics by JOHNNY MARKS
Arranged by LLOYD CONLEY

00868011

ROCKIN' AROUND THE CHRISTMAS TREE

VIOLIN 2
String Orchestra Arrangement

Music and Lyrics by JOHNNY MARKS
Arranged by LLOYD CONLEY

00868011

JINGLE-BELL ROCK

Words and Music by
JOE BEAL and JIM BOOTHE
Arranged by LLOYD CONLEY

VIOLIN 1
String Orchestra Arrangement

Medium Rock

JINGLE-BELL ROCK

Words and Music by
JOE BEAL and JIM BOOTHE
Arranged by LLOYD CONLEY

VIOLIN 2
String Orchestra Arrangement

00868011

SILVER BELLS

From the Paramount Picture THE LEMON DROP KID

**Words and Music by
JAY LIVINGSTON and RAY EVANS**
Arranged by LLOYD CONLEY

VIOLIN 1
String Orchestra Arrangement

00868011

SILVER BELLS
From the Paramount Picture THE LEMON DROP KID

VIOLIN 2
String Orchestra Arrangement

Words and Music by
JAY LIVINGSTON and RAY EVANS
Arranged by LLOYD CONLEY

00868011

LET IT SNOW! LET IT SNOW! LET IT SNOW!

VIOLIN 1
String Orchestra Arrangement

Words by SAMMY CAHN
Music by JULE STYNE
Arranged by LLOYD CONLEY

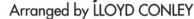

LET IT SNOW! LET IT SNOW! LET IT SNOW!

Violin 2
String Orchestra Arrangement

Words by SAMMY CAHN
Music by JULE STYNE
Arranged by LLOYD CONLEY

WHITE CHRISTMAS

From the Motion Picture Irving Berlin's HOLIDAY INN

VIOLIN 1
String Orchestra Arrangement

Words and Music by
IRVING BERLIN
Arranged by LLOYD CONLEY

WHITE CHRISTMAS
From the Motion Picture Irving Berlin's HOLIDAY INN

VIOLIN 2
String Orchestra Arrangement

Words and Music by
IRVING BERLIN
Arranged by LLOYD CONLEY